WATTS CHAPEL

WATTS CHAPEL

A Guide to the Symbols of Mary Watts's Arts and Crafts Masterpiece

Mark Bills

PHILIP WILSON PUBLISHERS

Compton Cemetery Chapel.

© Watts Gallery 2010
Text © Mark Bills

www.wattsgallery.org.uk

First published in 2010 by

Philip Wilson Publishers Ltd.
109 Drysdale Street
The Timber Yard
London N1 6ND

www.philip-wilson.co.uk

Distributed throughout the world
(excluding North America) by

I.B. Tauris & Co. Ltd.
6 Salem Road
London W2 4BU

Distributed in North America by

Palgrave Macmillan,
a division of St Martin's Press
175 Fifth Avenue
New York NY 10010

ISBN: 978-0-85667-692-5 (paperback)

Designed by Arnoud Verhaeghe
Edited by David Hawkins
Printed and bound in China by Everbest

All contemporary images © Anne Purkiss 2010.
All vintage photographs are property of the Watts Gallery Archive.

CONTENTS

FOREWORD

A visit to the Watts Chapel in 1989 was my first introduction to the extraordinary and unique Watts legacy of buildings and monuments in Compton. Walking up to the chapel through the yews was a gentle journey towards the complete surprise of this luminescent red terracotta building glowing in the late evening sun of a June day. There on the hillside in a small hollow off the Hogs Back, I had no concept of the wonder, delight and discovery that lay within. The combination of styles, the sense of place, and the purpose, strength and accessibility of the imagery made it an unforgettable experience and started my Watts journey!

A building so strongly based on such positive fundamental concepts and images of darkness turning into light, that displays the four friezes of hope, truth, love and life, provides imagery of the River of Life and the Tree of Life, and above all reinforces the message of resurrection, renewal and everlasting life, is a building that brings energy and hope, as well as surprise and delight, to many. Today, visitors from across the world as well as from Compton itself seek the peace, reflection and inspiration offered by the angels, symbolism and atmosphere of the Watts Cemetery Chapel. Its creation by over seventy local people and the involvement of local children in making the flowers give it a definite sense of place and represent a living commitment to art for all – one of the cornerstones of G.F. and Mary Seton Watts's beliefs.

I am very grateful to Mark Bills, curator of Watts Gallery, who regularly makes the pilgrimage from the gallery to the chapel to open it and review its conservation, for studiously revealing the thinking and inspiration behind this part of our Watts legacy. Through his series of *Studies into the Art of G.F. Watts* we have been able to rediscover the ideas, motivation and achievement of the great master. This book helps us, in a fascinating and practical way, to discover the depth, art, passion and purpose of Mary Watts, taking us step by step through the symbols and meanings of this remarkably ornate and detailed monument.

Once visitors or mourners pass through the chapel door watched over by angels looking downwards in sympathy and upwards in hope, and as they hear the chapel bell, with its inscription devised by G.F. Watts, 'Be my voice neither feared not forgotten', on leaving, they may wish to return, with this book in hand, to enjoy the comfort and encouragement offered by Mary Watts through this symbolic masterpiece.

Perdita Hunt
Director of Watts Gallery

Compton, Cemetery Chapel and Luchgate

PREFACE

This new book and guide to Mary Watts's Cemetery Chapel in Compton arises out of a need to introduce more easily, fully and systematically the rich body of symbols that decorate it. Mary Watts (1849–1938), its creator, was very much aware of this need and wrote a book entitled *The Word in the Pattern* for this purpose. The difference between her excellent book, which forms the basis of this guide, and the present one is two-fold: firstly, this includes many of the sources of the symbols that Mary drew from, particularly where she is unclear about the meaning of a particular symbol; and secondly, and more importantly, it is richly illustrated and arranged as simply as possible to clarify which symbols are being discussed. It is in effect a key to the symbols of the building as Mary Watts understood them. Written descriptions with few illustrations can only be fully absorbed with many hours spent at the chapel, book in hand, deciphering which description matches which detail from the intertangled body of images. The aim of this book is to overcome this problem so it can be an easily usable reference as well as serving as an overall guide to the building. To Mary a symbol was a 'magic key' that 'unlocks a door into a world of enchantment'. Ultimately, it is hoped that this guide will enhance both the understanding and enjoyment of this wonderful building.

Compton, Cemetery Chapel.

ACKNOWLEDGEMENTS

Producing a book is always reliant on a large number of people – from those who have added their knowledge of the subject to those who have worked on it. I must begin by acknowledging the work of Veronica Franklin Gould, whose championing of Mary Watts and the Watts Chapel has greatly aided our appreciation of it. She wrote the first guide, which is still in print and complements this present publication. Without Desna Greenhow this book would not have been written, and discussions with her about the symbolism have been invaluable. I would also like to thank Louise Boreham, Gail Naughton, Janet Lee, Hilary Underwood and Hilary Calvert for their knowledge and their love and enthusiasm for the Watts Cemetery Chapel. Thanks go to the Compton Cemetery Committee, and particularly the chair Marian Williams and Chris Harvey, for their continued work on preserving the chapel; to Anne Purkiss for photographing the chapel in sub-zero conditions; and to Malcolm and Barry Hodgson for building her scaffolding. I would also like to thank Catherine Hilary for her work on this book, Colin Grant and those at Philip Wilson Publishers. I am most grateful to Rob Fish and Martin Warner, Bishop of Whitby, for helping to interpret the symbolism, and finally thanks go to all those who care for the building, and its enormous number of supporters who know its value.

Photographic Acknowledgements
Colour photography is by Anne Purkiss. All other images are from the Watts Gallery Archive.

Watts Gallery is deeply grateful to all its generous donors and benefactors including:

An Anonymous Donor
The Art Fund
Billmeir Charitable Trust
The Deborah Loeb Brice Foundation
Hamish Dewar Ltd
Professor Rob Dickins CBE
John Ellerman Foundation
English Heritage
Esmée Fairbairn Foundation
The Fenton Arts Trust
Finnis Scott Foundation
Christopher Forbes
Foundation for Sport and the Arts
Foyle Foundation
The Robert Gavron Charitable Trust
J. Paul Getty Jnr Charitable Trust
The Isabel Goldsmith Patino Foundation
Guildford Borough Council
Peter Harrison Foundation
The Derek Hill Foundation
The Ingram Trust
KPMG Foundation
The Geoffrey and Carole Lawson Charitable Trust
John Lewis
The Linbury Trust
The George John and Sheilah Livanos Charitable Trust
Man Group plc Charitable Trust
The Michael Marks Charitable Trust
The Mercers' Company
The Henry Moore Foundation
Richard Ormond CBE
David Pike
The Pilgrim Trust
Restoration Fund
Rothschild Foundation
Sir Siegmund Warburg Voluntary Settlement
The Wates Foundation
Garfield Weston Foundation
Wolfson Foundation

INTRODUCTION

Watts Cemetery Chapel: *beautiful if translated by its accepted meaning in symbolism*[1]

Compton's Cemetery Chapel, which stands on the side of Budburrow Hill, is a Grade I listed building owned by the parish. It was consecrated by the Bishop of Winchester on 1 July 1898 and continues to be a working cemetery chapel. Most who visit it today, however, are there to admire its extraordinary design and decoration. Responses are mixed, but most are overwhelmed by this decoration, the astonishing body of images and symbols that appear on the outside in terracotta and on the inside in painted gesso. For many it provides a place for reflection and peace, which its creator Mary Watts (1849–1938) would, I am sure, have thoroughly approved of. It was built, she writes in the opening lines of her book *The Word in the Pattern*, 'to the loving memory of all who find rest near its walls, and for the comfort and help of those to whom the sorrow of separation yet remains'.[2]

It is difficult to know when exactly Mary conceived the idea of designing, building and decorating a chapel, but it must have come soon after her move to their Compton winter residence, Limnerslease, in 1891. In her biography of G.F. Watts, Mary notes:

> A new interest had grown up for us both in the last two years, the building of a chapel for the new village burial-ground, his gift to Compton. He did not design it, but suggested that, if we proposed to hold a class, the people of Compton might like to come to it and be taught to make simple patterns to decorate the walls; so that by this means a special and personal interest in the new graveyard would be acquired by the workers.[3]

The year 1895 was important for the start of the Thursday-night evening classes to train those who would make the chapel's decorations. It was also the year that the model for it was built and the land purchased. G.F. Watts's early biographer, Hugh Macmillan, wrote:

> For the expenses of the building and the laying out of the grounds around it, Watts provided the money which he earned by painting some special picture for it. But the chief work of carving, designing, and superintending the erection of the building was done by Mrs Watts to whom her husband invariably attributes all the credit. She was helped by Mr George Redmayne, an architect, who overlooked the practical work of erecting the building.[4]

The building and its outer decoration were completed for the chapel's consecration in 1898, and the interior was effectively finished on 15 April 1904, two weeks after the opening of Watts Gallery, with the installation of G.F. Watts's painting, *The All-Pervading*.

To accredit the work of building and creating the whole chapel wholly to Mary is, as Louise Boreham has argued, an exaggeration.[5] The success of the building, architecturally, must go in a great part to George Tunstal Redmayne FRIBA (1840–1912), a distinguished architect who was then semi-retired in Haselmere but had been an assistant to Alfred Waterhouse RA. As he is only mentioned in passing in texts about the chapel and, in *The Word in the Pattern*, only for designing the doors, he has been forgotten. This is not to undermine Mary's achievement, nor the contribution of the village. Mary was the artistic force behind the project and the creator of the chapel's

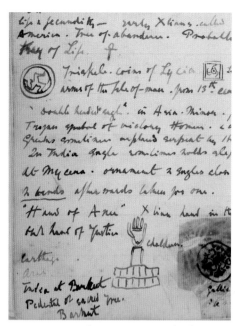

A page of Mary Watts's notebook

rich imagery and symbolism about which this book is concerned. Her elaborate notebook and writings on the chapel reveal the importance of the meanings of the building and how this was to be expressed in visual imagery. She is the artist.

The aim of the building was to be a mortuary chapel and a place for requiems, spiritual remembrance, comfort and inspiration. It is ambitious in its scope, reflecting the ideals that she shared with her husband G.F. Watts. She wrote:

> The chapel for the new graveyard in Compton has on its walls the story, or at least some fragments of the story, of the spiritual life, on the wing of which, in the passage between the mystery of birth and the mystery of death, material life is lifted to the glorious consciousness of its affinity with the Infinite.[6]

She was clearly influenced by her husband's philosophy and imagery, but her work was essentially very different in its approach. It drew on existing symbols that she refreshed in her own designs, for she believed that certain visual motifs had a universal and eternal meaning:

These signs, simple enough in themselves, come to us through the ages, bearing with them not only their deep spiritual meaning and suggestions, but being also witnesses of the eternity of religious aspiration; the inarticulate cry of the spirit of the human, seeking then, and now, and always, a return to its own source in the Divine Faith.[7]

The chapel reflected the meaning and forms of earlier ages translated into a late nineteenth-century Arts and Crafts masterpiece. Its shape is drawn from the Byzantine Greek cross, while its entrance is Celtic Romanesque. The Byzantine model and its reference to the Holy Sepulchre combine meaning and form. The decoration was inspired first and foremost by Mary's strong interest in Celtic design:

> In trying to revive in some degree that living quality which was in all decoration when patterns had meaning, the character of our own Celtic art – ancient British, Irish and Scotch as it is – has been followed, and many of the symbols are taken from carved stones and crosses, or from those rare and exquisite illuminations on vellum, now the treasures of national museums and libraries, but once the most sacred possessions of the Celts, who with devoted labour loved thus to make beautiful their manuscript books of the Gospels.[8]

Celtic forms and images from Irish and Scottish stone crosses and the Book of Kells are in evidence all over the building.[9] In this Mary could be said to be part of the Celtic Revival movement that was evident in so much Arts and Crafts work being created at the time. When she first saw the Lindisfarne Gospels at the British Museum she wrote:

> It takes one's breath away to think of all that devouring love of beautifying and enriching the

book as the holy man poured [sic] over it and wrought these marvellous lines & coloured in that delicate tender way his beautiful devices – under the magnifying glass only can one realize what the finish & perfection was.[10]

For the chapel's meaning Mary turned to the reasons for its creation and drew particularly from the symbolism of early Christian art. In a letter to the textile and dyestuffs manufacturer Sir James Morton (1867–1943) she noted the sources of her understanding of this symbolism and acknowledged 'Lord Lindsay whose book on Christian art was one of my great helps when I first thought of trying to make out the meaning in the old patterns'.[11] In the letter Mary refers to a number of works that were clearly influential on the formation of the chapel's rich symbolism, one of which was Lord Lindsay's *Sketches of the History of Christian Art* (1847). The overall symbolism of this consecrated Anglican chapel reflects less a particular denomination than an ecumenical and all-embracing Christianity, looking to the early church and using imagery from the eastern and western church traditions. Macmillan reflected:

> Though founded upon the great central truths of the Christian faith, it does not express any accepted dogmas of religion, but enforces only the universal laws of justice, charity and love, and is so broad and catholic in its teaching that it should conciliate even the most divergent ecclesiastical sects.[12]

Mary knew that her carefully planned symbolism would not be immediately open to all who saw it: it was 'exoteric and esoteric in its character, being in some instances so plain and simple that the most uneducated can understand it at once, and in others so hidden and intricate'.[13] In order to make its meaning plain to all, she wrote *The Word in the Pattern*, which explains in detail many of the decorative symbols. This often overlooked book is the main source of the current

guide to the chapel and enables Mary's intentions to be elucidated. But it was also the necessary to present this information afresh, including some of the texts and images that she drew from. The Bible is a primary source, particularly the writings of St John (in both the Gospel and Revelation) and his theology of the Logos, or Word of God, which is referred to in the title of Mary's book. Biblical references and allusions have been included as have the works that explained and formed her ideas of early Christian and Celtic art. Many of these are listed in her letter to James Morton, and the most important, J.R. Allen's *Early Christian Symbolism* (1887), W. & G. Audsley's *A Handbook of Christian Symbolism* (1865), W. Brindley and W.S. Weatherley's *Ancient Sepulchral Monuments* (1887), Lord Lindsay's *Sketches of the History of Christian Art* (1847) and Margaret Stokes's *Early Christian Art in Ireland* (1887), are referenced throughout the text in abbreviated form. These are particularly useful in finding the meanings that are not fully explained by Mary, as well as the visual sources from which she derived many of her images. Of course, Mary was a creative artist, and although the influence in some cases is very clear, in others it is less so. Macmillan observed: 'The symbolism on all of them is extremely elaborate, and much of it is purely original; but it is all combined in the most harmonious manner to carry out the moral teaching of the building.'[14]

Notes

1. Mary Watts, *The Word in the Pattern*, London 1905, p. 26.

2. Ibid., p. 3.

3. Mary Watts, *George Frederic Watts: The Annals of an Artist's Life*, 3 vols., London 1912, vol. II, p. 284.

4. Hugh Macmillan, *The Life-Work of George Frederick Watts R.A.*, London 1903, pp. 62–63.

5. Louise Boreham, 'Compton Chapel', *The Victorian: Magazine of the Victorian Society*, no. 3, March 2000, pp. 10–13.

6. Mary Watts, *The Word in the Pattern*, p. 3.

7. Ibid., p. 5.

8. Ibid., p. 3.

9. Mary could have studied this in detail in John Obadiah Westwood, *Fac-similies of the Miniatures and Ornaments of Anglo-Saxon and Irish Manuscripts*, London 1868.

10. Mary Watts, diary entry for 9 September 1896, Watts Gallery Archive.

11. Mrs Watts, letter to James Morton, 15 March 1901, James Morton Papers, National Archive of Art and Design, National Art Library, Victoria and Albert Museum, NRA28681 AAD 4-1978. Many thanks to Louise Boreham for drawing my attention to this.

12. Hugh Macmillan, *The Life-Work of George Frederick Watts R.A.*, p. 66.

13. Ibid.

14. Ibid., p. 67.

Well Head in Compton Cemetery.

CHRONOLOGY

1894, 25 May
Compton Parish Council resolved to purchase 'Grass Land on Budburrow Hill for the purpose of a New Cemetery'.

1895
A cardboard model made and Mary finishes the design by 9 August when she discusses it with the architect George Redmayne FRIBA.

1895, 2 October
Compton Parish Council pays William More Molyneux of Loseley £74 7s for the three-quarter acre ribbon of Budburrow Hill.

1895, 4 November
Mary opens her home for the first of her Thursday-evening Terra Cotta Home Arts classes.

1896
Mary is granted permission to sink a well at the cemetery's northern edge in March.

1897
Decorations for the chapel are exhibited at the annual Home Arts and Industries exhibition held in the circular upper gallery of the Albert Hall.

1898
Building and exterior decoration completed. The chapel doors are exhibited at the annual Home Arts and Industries exhibition held in the circular upper gallery of the Albert Hall.

1898, 1 July
The chapel is consecrated by the Bishop of Winchester, Randall Davidson.

1898, 24 December
Andrew and May Hichens hold a party on behalf of Compton Parish Council to thank the Wattses for their generous gift of the chapel.

1899
Altar design at the annual Home Arts and Industries exhibition held in the circular upper gallery of the Albert Hall.

1904, 15 April
A small version of *The All-Pervading* by G.F. Watts is hung over the altar, completing the decoration of the interior.

1904, 1 July
Death of G.F. Watts whose ashes are placed in the chapel in a casket designed by Thomas Wren.

PLAN OF THE CHAPEL

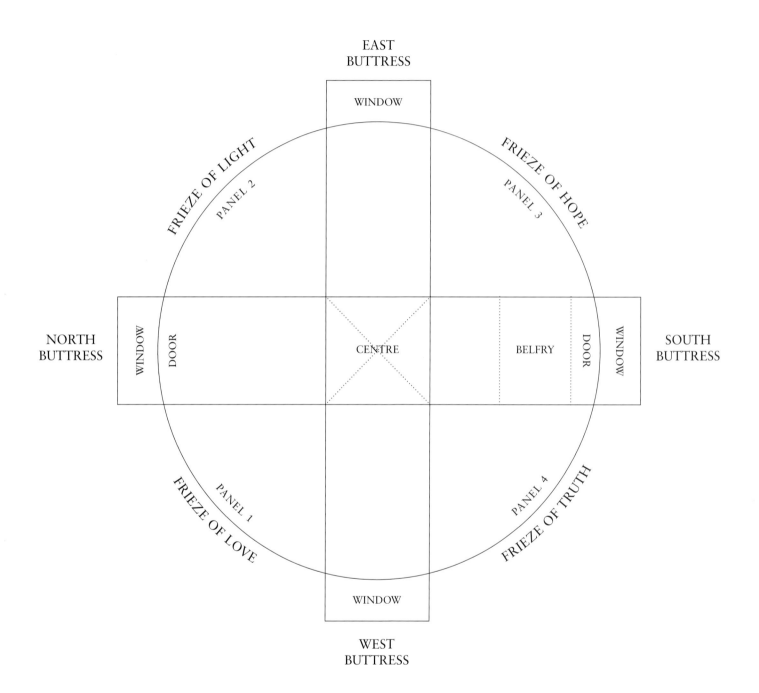

EAST
BUTTRESS

WINDOW

FRIEZE OF LIGHT

PANEL 2

FRIEZE OF HOPE

PANEL 3

NORTH
BUTTRESS

WINDOW

DOOR

CENTRE

BELFRY

DOOR

WINDOW

SOUTH
BUTTRESS

PANEL 1

FRIEZE OF LOVE

PANEL 4

FRIEZE OF TRUTH

WINDOW

WEST
BUTTRESS

ENTRANCE ARCH & DOOR

I. EXTERIOR

1. Shape and Design

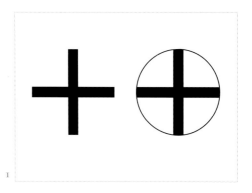

Ancient origins

Mary ascribed many of her symbols to ancient sources in the belief that they revealed deep universal truths, which for Mary were more significantly explained with their Christian meaning.

The Circle of Eternity, with the Cross of Faith running through it, is from pre-historic times. The earliest Christians found this sign sacred among men struggling to find, like the men of Ephesus, the 'Unknown God,' [Acts 17:23] and they gave to it the consecration of the fuller revelation of the Christian faith. If the cross has been used in past ages as a symbol of power over the earth, it was more to them; it was the power of redeeming Love, with arms outstretched to all the world. If it meant to others the path of the swift sun in its course, shining over four quarters, – that path of glory that led men to cry in the oldest language of the world [Mary takes this to mean Sanskrit] to the 'Light Father' – it was more to them, it was the sign of the Divine speaking to the human saying 'I am Light of the World, he that followeth me shall not walk in darkness, but shall have the Light of Life,' [John 8:12] and the circle running round this sign of love and light and life, complete it with the sign of eternity; being as it were a promise of these perfected and immortal. So do these signs, simple enough in themselves, come to us through the ages, bearing with them, not only their deep spiritual meanings and suggestions, but being also witnesses of the eternity of religious aspiration. (Watts, pp. 4–5)

The Christian cemetery chapel

Following the Byzantine model, the chapel design uses the shape of a Greek cross, [Fig.1] with its limbs of equal length (Audsley, pp. 67–68). Characteristically, a Byzantine church has 'four naves … of equal length and breadth … while in the centre a Dome or Cupola soared upwards, expanding, as it were, into infinity like the vault of heaven' (Lindsay, vol. I, pp. 62–63).

Being a cemetery chapel, it is modelled more specifically on the Church of the Holy Sepulchre in Jerusalem, [Fig.2] where it is believed Christ was crucified and buried before His resurrection. As such it is symbolic of both death and resurrection, while the never-ending circle without beginning or end, a symbol found throughout the chapel and in particular at the very top of the dome, represents everlasting life. 'The building, in its form, is also linked', Mary notes, with 'the Church of the Holy Sepulchre' and with round churches

> built in England [examples survive in Cambridge, Northampton and London] … Of the buildings at Jerusalem, built by the Emperor Constantine, at the suggestion of his mother, to commemorate the Passion, the Crucifixion, and the Resurrection, and consecrated to sacred uses in AD 335, it is interesting to notice that the round church, built over what was believed to be the site of the Holy Sepulchre, was called Anastasis, or Resurrection, for not the thought of death, but the thought of life, the promise of life eternal, was to be suggested by these walls. (Watts, pp. 24–25)

The setting of the chapel on a hill also echoes this link, and as in all traditional chapels the altar faces east towards Jerusalem with a highly decorated entrance at the western end.

2. The Entrance

The entrance in the western side of the chapel with its semicircular arch supported by three pillars on each side takes it design from Celtic Romanesque and, more particularly, early Irish churches such as Clonfert Cathedral, County Galway, and those illustrated in Margaret Stokes's *Early Christian Art in Ireland* [Fig.3] (Stokes 1887, Part II, pp. 66–81).

i. Frieze, archway and pillars

The 'Garment of Praise' friezes: consolation and salvation

The two identical friezes [Fig.4] on either side of the entrance arch represent an embroidered hanging into which symbols are woven. Taking the words of John Ruskin (1819–1900) from *The Stones of Venice*, Mary describes them as forming a 'wall veil' and, more specifically, a 'garment of praise'. The source is Isaiah 61: 'The garment of praise for the spirit of heaviness' (Isaiah 61:3)

FIGS. 95, 96.—MOULDINGS ON DOORWAYS, KILLESHIN.

3

FIG. 103.—DOORWAY, FRESHFORD.

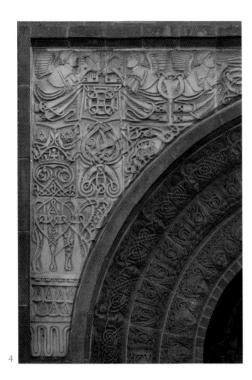

'To bind up the broken hearted' [Fig.6] (Isaiah 61:1), represented by the 'binding up the heart' (Watts, p. 14).

'To proclaim liberty to the captives' [Fig.7] (Isaiah 61:1), illustrated by 'loosing the chains' (Watts, p. 14).

and 'I will greatly rejoice in the LORD, my soul shall be joyful in my God; for he hath clothed me with the garments of salvation, he hath covered me with the robe of righteousness, as a bridegroom decketh himself with ornaments, and as a bride adorneth herself with her jewels' (Isaiah 61:10). The decoration reflects the book of Isaiah in its praise of God and the prophet's confident forecast that all will be made well. The words of consolation and salvation are particularly fitting to a cemetery chapel. Each of the symbols illustrates the following lines from chapter 61:

'Good tidings unto the meek' [Fig.5] (Isaiah 61:1), symbolized by the 'Star of Hope and crown of the meek' (Watts, p. 14).

'To comfort all that mourn' [Fig.8] (Isaiah 61:2), represented by seven lamps, which are associated with the Jewish menorah (a seven-branched candlestick), but more specifically here with the seven gifts of the Holy Spirit. The gifts of the spirit are more typically represented by seven doves, but here Mary uses seven burning lamps. (Audsley, p. 49). The source is Isaiah:

And the spirit of the LORD shall rest upon him, the spirit of wisdom and understanding, the spirit of counsel and might, the spirit of knowledge and of the fear of the LORD; And shall make him of quick understanding in the fear of the LORD: and he shall not judge after the sight of his eyes, neither reprove after the hearing of his ears. (Isaiah 11:2–3)

Mary uses a Middle English source such as Richard Rolle of Hampole (*c.* 1300–49) and his 'Seuene Gyftes of ye Haly Gaste' in noting 'the seven lamps of the Spirit (the Comforter) which are: "Ye gifte of wisdome [Wisdom], ye gifte of pittie [Piety], ye gifte of strengthe [Fortitude], ye gift of comfait [Knowledge], ye gifte of understandinge [Understanding], ye gifte of counyinge [Council], ye gifte of dreede [Fear of the Lord]"' (Watts, p. 14).

'To give unto them beauty from ashes' [Fig.9] (Isaiah 61:3), symbolized by 'the Phoenix rising from the flames' (Watts, p. 14).

'The oil of joy for mourning' [Fig.10] (Isaiah 61:3), represented by 'oil vessels, shaped as lachrymals

or tear bottles; the interlacing cord here becomes the olive branch in sign of victory and peace, the oil for the consecration' (Watts, p. 14).

'The garment of praise for the spirit of heaviness' [Fig.11] (Isaiah 61:3), symbolized by angels and trumpets:

The praising angels; below them the trumpets which bear the symbol of day and night ('the red day and the black day' – Rig Veda), very often found on the Celtic crosses, and carried down to this day, over the doors of wayside inns, where, in the name of 'The Chequers,' this sign of the hospitality of the old hostel still lingers. (Watts, p. 14)

At the apex of the arch is 'a Celtic monogram for the Sanctus or Holy, Holy, Holy! With the wings of the Spirit on either side' [Fig.12] (Watts, p. 14) Other decorations that form parts of the frieze represent the River of Life and the Cross of Faith with hearts. [Fig.13]

13

15

16

14

The archway

The three-tiered arch shows in turn fifteen angels' heads, peacock feathers and a Celtic knot of inter-laced hearts. [Fig.14] Mary expressed it:

> From the supported columns the archway rises with the choir of angels; angels looking down-ward in sympathy or upward in hope. In their feathers is the peacock's eye, the old symbol of watchfulness, and interlaced with them the cord of unity, ending with a beautiful knot often found upon Celtic crosses where the cord traces four hearts interlaced, so as to give at the same time the sign of the cross, sacrificing love; love not for one, but for all, even to the four quarters of the earth – Divine love, sacrificing, suffering, to give spiritual life. (Watts, p. 13)

Angels looking up in hope or down in sympathy. [Fig.15]

Peacock feathers and eyes. [Fig.16]

Celtic knot made of four hearts. [Fig.17]

The pillars: God and resurrection in the parables of nature

The arch is supported by three pillars or columns on each side. [Fig.18] The central column contains the words 'I AM' in the form of a monogram. This refers to God the creator and appears in the book of Exodus when 'God said unto Moses, I AM THAT I AM' (Exodus 3:14). The 'I AM' is also important in referring to Christ and the 'I am' sayings of Jesus which appear in the Gospel of St John: 'I am the bread of life' or 'living bread' (6:35, 51); 'I am the light of the world' (8:12, 9:5); 'I am the door' (10:11, 14); 'I am the

good shepherd' (10:11, 14); 'I am the resurrection and the life' (11:25); 'I am the way, the truth and the life' (14:6); and 'I am the true vine' (15:1, 5). All these sayings have echoes throughout the decoration of the chapel. The name of Christ and the letters alpha and omega are interwoven throughout these pillars: 'I am Alpha and Omega, the beginning and the ending, saith the Lord' (Revelation 1:8).

The interlacing cord of Celtic art [Fig.19] is 'used as a symbol of the unity of a divine life and law, running through all things' (Watts, p. 11). Interwoven with the letter 'I' is an image of a hand within a halo or nimbus, which Mary refers to as 'the Celtic Symbol of God the Creator' (Watts, p. 11). In her chapel notebook she illustrates the hand of God emerging from a cloud and framed by a nimbus with a Greek cross.

This symbol, [Fig.20] known as the Dextera Dei, appears 'upon two high crosses of Ireland, namely, that of Muiredach at Monasterboice, and that of King Fland at Clonmacnois. In both cases the hand is surrounded by a nimbus' (Allen, pp. 163–64), and these appear to be the main source, even though 'this symbol is used throughout the whole range of early Christian art to express the First Person of the Trinity' (Allen, p. 161).

The two columns that flank the 'I AM' column are made up of six separate images. [Fig.18] These are repeated on each side apart from one, making a total of seven separate designs. They consist of a single kneeling figure, who, according to Mary, is 'reverently interpreting parables from the book of nature, that tell him of life after death' (Watts, p. 11). The theme of resurrection is illustrated in examples from nature where life arises from death. St John expressed it: 'Verily, verily, I say unto you, Except a corn of wheat fall into the ground and die, it abideth alone: but if it die, it bringeth forth much fruit' (John 12:24). Each of the images follows Mary's order:

21

'No. 1 The young blade springing from the dry seed, seemingly dead and buried. "Thou fool, that which thou sowest is not quickened unless it die"' [Fig.21] (1 Corinthians 15:36; Watts, p. 11).

22

'No. 2 The butterfly rising with shining wings from its little tomb, the chrysalis' [Fig.22] (Watts, p. 11).

23

'No. 3 The flower in full faith casting off its petals that the seed may ripen, and once more renew life' [Fig.23] (Watts, p. 12).

24

'No. 4 The human heart, owning to itself its spiritual birthright' [Fig.24] (Watts, p. 12). 'Man looketh on the outward appearance, but the Lord looketh on the heart' (1 Samuel 16:7).

25

'No. 5 The flower that closes with the setting sun, and opens again when darkness is past' [Fig.25] (Watts, p. 12).

26

'No. 6 The stars in their courses, that most splendid page in all the Book of Nature' [Fig.26] (Watts, p. 12). The image of three stars evokes the Trinity, drawing from the Book of Kells, and refers to the systems of the universe. Mary uses scientific theories to explain how the universe reveals God and resurrection. She quotes the famous words of Johannes Kepler (1571–1630) as he was formulating his Laws of Planetary Motion: 'Oh God! I am thinking Thy thoughts after Thee.' Less well known is the theory of stars being created from the shattered fragments of other stars to illustrate resurrection in nature. This is taken from the 'meteoritic hypothesis' that Sir Joseph Norman Lockyer (1836–1920), astronomer and journal editor, developed in the late 1870s. In it he attempted to explain how stars evolved from a large body of meteorites. 'If this be so,' Mary writes, 'then the parable of life and death and rebirth is written in the great firmament of heaven.' (Watts, p. 12)

27

'No. 7 On the right side of the doorway where these symbols are otherwise repeated, there is a parable from our own earth, Light, Twilight, and Night. In loneliness the human heart still asks

Watchman, what of the night? And the answering cry is still "The morning cometh." In the shadow of the globe lies another comforting simile, in as much as there is night only over one-third part of the earth, while two-thirds are always in the light.' [Fig.27] (Watts, pp. 12–13)

28

ii. The doors

The great doors of the chapel were prepared in chestnut and oak and carved by the Compton wheelwright Thomas Steadman. [Fig.28] The door's metalwork was designed by the architect George Redmayne and forged by the village blacksmith Clarence Sex for a fee of £21 5s. It was exhibited at the 1898 annual Home Arts and Industries exhibition held in the circular upper gallery of the Albert Hall. 'Amongst a capital display by Mrs Watts's Compton class,' the *Daily News* reported, was 'a massive oaken door', while an undecorated door was temporarily put in its place (*Daily News*, 19 May 1898). The overall form and style of carving are reminiscent of early Scandinavian door carvings, such as the carved wooden door from Valthiofstad Church, Iceland (illustrated in J. Romilly Allen, 'Early Scandinavian Wood-Carvings, Part II', *The Studio*, 1897, p. 83). Mary notes:

> The carved cross behind the wrought iron cross on the door of the chapel, is copied from a grave stone at Iona, in Argyleshire [Brindley & Weatherley, plate 102], and evidently a transcription from rude wicker work or 'wattle,' links this building with the first Christianity of Britain, when from rude churches built of wattle our forefathers' voices rose … They very possibly used such a cross, woven in wattle, as a symbol of their faith. (Watts, p. 24)

30

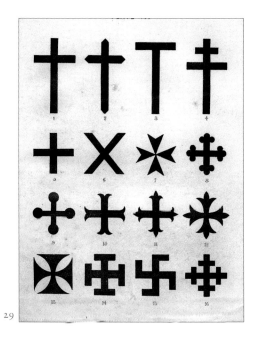

29

The symbolism of the doors includes several crosses, a familiar Latin crucifix, a Greek cross of faith dissecting the circle of eternity like the building itself, a 'Tau' cross that resembles the Greek letter 'T', and the Patriarchal cross with two cross beams. [Fig.29] (Audsley, pp. 65–71). In the upper section of the doors 'behind the cross on the door there is a glimpse through a circle into light; circle within circle, with flames and wings – eternity, mystery, light, motion, spirituality, protection' (Watts, p. 25).

The top section is presented as 'ruling above the mystery of darkness; the dragon below, smitten through by the cross' (Watts, pp. 24–25). [Fig.30] The image of the dragon is familiar in many cultures and in all periods of Christian art 'as the symbol of the Evil Spirit' (Audsley, p. 143). This was derived from Revelation: 'And the great dragon was cast out, that old serpent, called the Devil, and Satan, which deceiveth the whole world: he was cast out into the earth, and his angels were cast out with him' (Revelation 12:9). Most familiarly, St Michael is shown overcoming the dragon, depicting the words of Revelation:

31

'And there was war in heaven: Michael and his angels fought against the dragon; and the dragon fought and his angels' (Revelation 12:7). An illustration in Allen of 'St Michael and the Dragon' at Hoveringham shows a dragon with its interwoven tails and wings. [Fig.31]

32

The exquisite ironwork depicts 'the cross of faith and key of eternal life, another link in the great chain of aspiration forged only of these little concrete signs, but stretching far down the ages from human heart to human heart, for its comforting, strengthening and uplifting God-ward' (Watts, p. 26). In the middle the wrought-iron ends include a Tau or 'Anticipatory' cross acting as a mast for sails on either side [Fig. 32] that represent the 'breath of life' (Watts, p. 26). This phrase derives from the Greek word *pneuma*, which means 'wind', 'breath' and 'spirit'. The billowing sail makes visible that which is invisible.

33

3. The Four Buttresses

The four 'buttresses', as Mary describes the limbs of the Greek cross, follow the orientations of the compass north, south, east and west, symbolically dividing the world in quarters (see photographs on pp. 2, 6, 7). Each has two windows at the end, which are divided by three columns with decorative capitals and bases. The designs on the sides of the buttresses are almost identical, although those on the capitals change positions. [Fig.33]

34

i. Front and windows

At the base of each column at the front of all four buttresses is a design taken from the Carew Cross in Wales. [Figs.34–36] This Celtic form is complex and maze-like, and according to Mary, 'the symbol was used by British Christians to signify the labyrinth or maze of life, round which was sometimes written the words, "God leadeth"' (Watts, p. 15). She takes the design to be made up of 'two very ancient symbols': the Tau cross and the swastika. The Tau or Anticipatory cross, evident in much of the chapel, is an ancient symbol, which for Mary was the sign 'painted on the door-posts by the Children of Israel when the destroying angel passed over' (Watts, p. 15) and was used by the ancient Egyptians as 'their sign of immortality, and called by them the Key of Life' (Watts, p. 15). The swastika (*suastika* or *svastika*) is an ancient symbol found in all the major eastern religions, Buddhism, Jainism and Hinduism. The word

35

from the Sanskrit is made up of *su*, meaning 'good', and *asti*, meaning 'to be', which combine as *svasti*, meaning 'well-being', and *ka*, intensifying it – in other words, an object of well-being, like a kind of a talisman. Its shape is widespread in both the east and west and was widely used as a symbol in Celtic and Old Norse art. Mary refers to it as a 'sign of beneficence, again over the four quarters, possibly the path of the sun' (Watts, p. 15). The famous lines by Robert Browning (1812–89), 'God's in His Heaven, All's right with the world', sum up the idea.

36

The two crosses (Tau and swastika) make up this labyrinth or maze of life, which 'may bewilder, but the path of light runs through it' (Watts, p. 15). Mary names this path 'It is Well', which is possibly a reference to the very famous hymn of the time, 'It is Well with My Soul', by Horatio Gates Spafford (1828–88). Life, or the path to life eternal, is seen as a complex pattern symbolized by the labyrinth in which 'God leadeth' (Watts, p. 15; Romans 2:4). Mary ends her description of these symbols with lines from the Spanish saint, St Teresa of Avila (1515–82), translated into English by Henry Wadsworth Longfellow (1807–82):

> Let nothing disturb thee,
> Nothing affright thee.
> All things are passing,
> God never changeth;
> Patient endurance
> Attaineth to all things,
> Who God possesseth
> In nothing is wanting;
> Alone God sufficeth.

37

The east and west buttress capitals are the same and represent the Trinity of Father, Son and Holy Ghost. [Fig.37] The theological conception of the three in one has traditionally been expressed through abstract designs, the triangle, the double triangle and three interwound circles. 'The doctrine of the Trinity', writes Audsley, 'is distinctly symbolised' by the equilateral triangle: 'the equality of its three component parts declares the perfect equality of the Persons of the Godhead, while the union of those parts speaks of the unity of the Godhead. The appropriateness of this geometrical form appears to have been acknowledged

38

by artists of all ages, and during the early centuries of the Church' (Audsley, p. 54). [Fig.38] The intersection of two triangles, which is the Star of David, thus declaring its Jewish roots, 'is commonly accepted as expressive of the infinity of the Trinity' (Audsley, p. 58). The three intersecting circles are similarly expressive of the Trinity and form an image of the trefoil or shamrock.

39

The words of St Paul, 'NOW THROUGH', 'A GLASS', 'DARKLY', [Fig.39] are written at the base of the three capitals: 'Now we see through a glass darkly; but then face to face: now I know in part; but then shall I know even also as I am known' (1 Corinthians 13:12).

The designs for the capitals on the north and south buttresses are different to those for the east

40

and west but also represent the Trinity of Father, Son and Holy Ghost. The Father (God) in the centre is represented by the hand (Dextera Dei) lifted in the sign of the blessing with the letters 'o Ω π'. [Fig.40]

41

The Son (Jesus Christ) is represented by the cross and circle with the letters 'I X C', which stand as the first and last letters of Jesus Christ in Greek: 'IHCOUC XPICTOC' (Iesous Christos). [Fig.41]

42

The Holy Spirit is represented as 'the Dove surrounded by the aureole' (Watts, p. 16). This traditional emblem is accompanied by the letters 'S S', which represent the first letter of the Latin Sanctus (Holy). [Fig.42] The words 'HOLY HOLY HOLY' are written at the base of the three capitals: 'Holy,

holy, holy, is the LORD of hosts: the whole earth is full of his glory' (Isaiah 6:3).

ii. Side and capitals

The Tree of Life

On each of the eight sides of the buttresses a vertical terracotta frieze in two sections depicts the Tree of Life, [Fig.33] an important image throughout the chapel: 'In very varied forms, down to the Middle Ages, the Tree of Life was a common pattern carved, painted or embroidered upon things used for sacred purposes in Cathedrals and Churches' (Watts, pp. 5–6). Mary learnt about this ancient symbol through the work of Professor Archibald Henry Sayce (1845–1933), Orientalist and philologist. He was a great popularizer of the importance of archaeology in understanding the Bible. His knowledge was prodigious and he was able to write in over twenty ancient and modern languages. Mary quotes an Akkadian (Babylonian) hymn written between three and four thousand years ago, translated by Sayce, which tells of the Tree of Life planted 'in a holy place ... unto the heart of its holy house, which spread its shade like a forest, there was none who within entered not' (Watts, p. 6). The Tree of Life appears in the Bible in the Garden of Eden, so Adam and Eve may 'eat, and live for ever' (Genesis 3:22), and when they were driven from paradise, God placed 'Cherubims, and a flaming sword which turned every way, to keep the way of the tree of life' (Genesis 3:24). It was suggested by Orientalists such as Sayce that the Garden of Eden was in ancient Babylon:

> The garden planted in Eden may have been near the town of Eridu, now marked by the ruins of Abu-Shahrein, in the south of Babylonia, which in the second millennium before the Christian era stood on the sea-shore. At all events, Eridu is regarded as a sacred city in Babylonian literature;

it is frequently termed 'the good' or 'holy,' and near it was a forest or 'garden' where grew 'the holy pine-tree' identified with 'the tree of life'. (George Smith, *The History of Babylonia*, ed. Revd A.H. Sayce, London 1884, p. 63)

The Tree of Life also appears in the Revelation of St John, which is the source for the image on the sides of the buttresses. The columns that frame it are also derived from the same source:

And he shewed me a pure river of water of life, clear as crystal, proceeding out of the throne of God and of the Lamb. In the midst of the street of it, and on either side of the river, was there the tree of life, which bare twelve manner of fruits, and yielded her fruit every month; and the leaves of the tree were for the healing of the nations. (Revelation 22:1–2)

Mary notes that 'on the decorated bricks that run up all the buttresses is the "Tree of Life," that mystic tree of St John's vision', where 'all creation' is symbolized through the twelve fruits (Watts, p. 5). These are presented as a hierarchy of creation from flowers on earth at the bottom to angels at the top, as follows:

1. Flowers [Fig.43]

2. Fruit [Fig.44]

3. Shells [Fig.45]

4. Fish [Fig.46]

5. Serpents [Fig.47]

48

6. Birds [Fig.48]

49

7. Beasts [Fig.49]

50

8. Man and woman [Fig.50]

51

9. The sun [Fig.51]

The symbol of the sun is from a Scandinavian bronze. In the centre is the triskele [three conjoined spirals, particularly used in Celtic art] or three steps of the sun, morning, noon and night, while the outer circle has the sign of the four quarters of the earth or points of the compass. (Watts, 2nd edition, p. 7)

52

10. The moon [Fig.52]

53

11. Stars [Fig.53]

54

12. Angels [Fig.54]

43

44

46

47

49

50

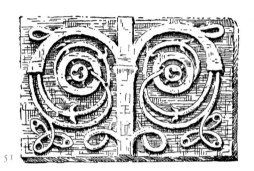

51

52

53

54

55

The fruits of the frieze are divided by a 'roof', [Fig.55] of which Mary writes:

> The lower buttress has upon its roof, the scalloped pattern in common use now, but in very early times (possibly by its inventors) it was only used when the ornament was meant to express the feeling of peace, and was probably suggested by the breast feathers of the mother bird, a simile made so beautiful and pathetic by the words, how often would I have gathered thy children together, even as a hen gathereth her chickens under her wings, and ye would not! [Matthew 23:37]. (Watts, pp. 10–11)

56

The columns on the sides of the buttresses are decorated with wavy lines [Fig.56] representing the River of Life. Mary also uses the theme of the River of Life on the wellhead at the end of the cemetery. Its panels show two angels, one carrying a symbol of the Tree of Life, the other a bowl of water for the Water of Life. The inscription on the wellhead reads: 'The Lord God planted a garden eastward in Eden, and a river went out of Eden to water the garden' (Genesis 2:8).

57

The right-hand side of the northern buttress bears a signature of one of the chapel's many workers: 'J. Head'. [Fig.57]

Capitals representing the Four Evangelists

Perhaps the most common symbols to be found in a church are those of the Four Evangelists who wrote the New Testament Gospels: Matthew, Mark, Luke and John. They are represented, in turn, by a winged man, a winged lion, a winged ox or calf, and an eagle, images derived from the Vision of Ezekiel and the Revelation of St John:

> Also out of the midst thereof came the likeness of four living creatures. (Ezekiel 1:5)

> Their wings were joined one to another; they turned not when they went; they went every one straight forward. As for the likeness of their faces, they four had the face of a man, and the face of a lion, on the right side: and they four had the face of an ox on the left side; they four also had the face of an eagle. (Ezekiel 1:9–10)

> And the first beast was like a lion, and the second beast like a calf, and the third beast had a face as a man, and the fourth beast was like a flying eagle. And the four beasts had each of them six wings about him. (Revelation 4:8)

'The writings of St Jerome, in the beginning of the 5th century, gave to artists authority for the appropriation of the four creatures to the Evangelists' (Audsley, p. 98). Their images are prolific in sacred art. Mary's capitals on the River of Life columns are clearly influenced by the Book of Kells, from which they are drawn. The eagle of St John is found throughout the chapel. Each Evangelist's symbol has a particular meaning in the life of Christ: Matthew represents Christ's birth as a man, or the Incarnation; Luke represents the Passion; Mark, the Resurrection; and John, Christ's Ascension into heaven.

58

St Matthew

'To St Matthew was given the creature in human likeness because he commences his holy Gospel with the human generation of Christ; and because in his writings the human nature of our Lord is more dwelt upon than the divine.' [Fig. 58] (Audsley, p. 98)

59

St Mark

'The creature in the form of a Lion was given to St Mark, because, in his Gospel, he sets forth the royal dignity of our Lord, and His power manifested in his Resurrection from the Dead. St Mark dwells upon the Resurrection of Christ and thereby claims the Lion, which … was accepted in early times as a symbol of the Resurrection. He also opens his Gospel with the mission of John the Baptist. "The voice of one crying in the wilderness," is appropriately figured by the Lion, whose roaring voice is heard in wilds and deserts.' [Fig. 59] (Audsley, p. 98)

 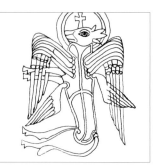

60

St Luke

'The creature in the form of an Ox was given to St Luke, because, in his Gospel he particularly dwells on the Atonement and Priesthood of our Lord. The Ox, the beast of sacrifice, fitly sets forth the sacred office and also the atonement for sin by blood.' [Fig. 60] (Audsley, pp. 98–99)

61

St John

'The creature in the form of an Eagle was given to St John, because, the Eagle soars on its powerful wings high towards heaven to contemplate the Divine nature of Christ and to bring back to earth revelations of sublime and awful mysteries.' [Fig. 61] (Audsley, p. 99)

4. The Path of the Just: Friezes Held by Corbels

Mary calls the friezes that run around the chapel exterior the 'Path of the Just', a phrase from the book of Proverbs: 'But the path of the just is as the shining light, that shineth more and more unto the perfect day' (Proverbs 4:18).

64

62

63

'The idea of the path,' Mary writes, 'is suggested by the tree-like pattern dividing the panels, in whose roots mice and small creeping things lodge,[Figs.62–63] while on the branches there Are Doves of peace, and storks, the symbol of the home' [Fig.64] (Watts, p. 17). The trees recall the passage, 'that they might be called trees of Righteousness, the planting of the Lord' (Isaiah 61:3). The path is made up of four friezes, representing in turn: Hope, Truth, Love and Light, which takes the viewer from faith and hope to enlightenment. The frieze starts with Hope at the back, southeast side of the chapel and goes in a circle clockwise through Truth, Love and Light.

Corbels

Each of the four friezes is supported by the same three corbels. Their subjects are taken from one of the 'I am' sayings of Jesus: 'I am the way, the truth and the life' (St John 14:6).

65

66

The Way is represented by the labyrinth or maze, [Figs.65–66] symbolizing the difficult spiritual journey through life. It is drawn from *Architecture, Mysticism and Myth* (1892) by William R. Lethaby (1857–1931), in particular an illustration in chapter VII, 'The Labyrinth', which Mary used as the model for this corbel.

67

68

The Truth is represented by a Scandinavian 'sun boat', a Viking ship with a setting sun behind its single mast. Like the metalwork on the doors, the boat has a Patriarchal cross as a mast, while the sails are blown by the breath of life. 'The Boat of the Sun,' as Mary describes it, 'with its symbol of day and night, chequers upon the boat's side; the sails, breath of life; the mast, the double-armed cross' [Figs.67–68] (Watts, p. 17).

The Life is represented by 'the vine, "the Christian's life in Christ", with its suggestion of a tree of life: "I am the Vine, ye are the Branches:

69

70

He that abideth in me, and I in him, the same bringeth forth much fruit: for without me ye can do nothing" [John 15:5].' [Figs.69–70] (Watts, p. 17)

Individual friezes representing Hope, Truth, Love, Light

Each of the friezes has a central panel with a symbolic bird that represents the frieze and is repeated on each side of the central cross. The Tau cross at the centre of the panel is made up of two wings and a central column. Each contains a circular symbol at its heart, making it look like a Latin cross. 'Four attendant spirits attend the symbols of those qualities and virtues which naturally and rightly follow these' (Watts, p. 18). These are depicted two on either side holding inscribed discs. The Path of the Just friezes take the viewer from Hope to Light through Truth and Love.

i. Frieze of the Spirit of Hope
(southeast side) [Figs.71–72]

'On the south-east section, the spirit of Hope rules.' (Watts, p. 18)

The symbolic bird

The bird of Hope is the peacock, which offers

> the hope of immortality, chosen because the poetic teachers who fixed our symbols, saw that those wonderful blue eyes surrounded by rays shining with the colour of light, were cast every

year and renewed again, and yet again; possibly too, because they saw the blind blue eye looked ever upwards to the heavens whilst it trailed along the earth. [Fig.72] (Watts, p. 18)

Audsley notes its importance as traditional Christian symbol:

> The Peacock was adopted in early times as an emblem of the Resurrection, because it yearly renewed its beautiful plumage, and sometimes an emblem of Immortality, because it was commonly believed to have incorruptible flesh. The use of the Peacock with its tail fully displayed, as an emblem of Pride and Worldly Pomp, is an introduction of a later age. (Audsley, pp. 88–89)

Mary also notes the sacred associations with Hinduism and Buddhism in her chapel notebook.

The central symbol

The central symbol is made up of the anchor, star and three types of cross – Latin, Patriarchal and Tau. 'The anchor of Hope', Mary writes, 'is over the four quarters of the earth' (Watts, p. 18). It is an early Christian symbol and 'used in Christian art at a very early period, being frequently found in the catacombs. It is the symbol of steadfast hope, firmness, tranquillity, and patience' (Audsley, p. 141). The anchor consists of the Patriarchal cross, one of the two 'Ecclesiastical Crosses ... distinguished from all others by the number of their traverse beams'. Of these, the Papal cross has three beams, while 'the lesser has two beams' and 'appears to have been first introduced in Greece, where it was generally adopted, doubtless as a sign of distinction. The name it bears in heraldry would imply as much, being termed the Patriarchal Cross.' (Audsley, p. 66.) According to Mary, this 'cross of Faith, for Hope and Faith cannot be dissevered, the Latin cross in this symbol, dates from a very early time, and the double arm is said to represent the scroll of Pilate' (Watts, p. 18). The centre of the cross is made up of a star: 'The star was given to Hope, no doubt because the evening star that shines out when the sun has gone down, and that is again the morning star that heralds dawn' (Watts, p. 18).

The four attendant spirits

The Spirits of Hope are the spider, lion, hart and dove.

73

The spider represents the patience of Hope (inscription: 'PATIENCE'). [Fig.73] 'The spider for the patience of Hope. "It is good that a man should both hope and wait" [Lamentations 3:26]' (Watts, p. 18).

The lion represents the courage of Hope (inscription: 'COURAGE'). [Fig.74] 'The lion is for the courage of Hope. "Be you of good courage all ye that hope in the Lord" [Psalm 31:24]' (Watts, p. 18).

74

75

The hart represents the aspiration or aim of Hope (inscription: 'AIM'), [Fig.75] taken from Psalm 42. 'The hart, the aspiration or aim of Hope, "As the hart panteth after the water-brooks so panteth my soul after Thee, oh God" [Psalms 42:1]. "Why art thou cast down, oh my soul, why art thou disquieted within me. Hope thou in God" [Psalms 43:5]' (Watts, p. 19).

76

The dove with a nimbus represents the comfort of Hope (inscription: 'COMFORT'). [Fig.76] Mary writes: 'The dove the comfort of Hope, the Spirit that "will not leave us comfortless" [*Book of Common Prayer*, Collect for the Sunday after Ascension Day]' (Watts, p. 18). 'The Dove was chosen as symbol, amongst birds,' Audsley writes,

77

because of 'its gentle and loving nature, in the first place, and [because] in the second, from the purity of its plumage, [it] has been preferably selected as the image of the Holy Ghost. Indeed, a white dove is regarded, both in historical narration and in works of art, as the impersonation of God.' (Audsley, p. 46.)

ii. Frieze of the Spirit of Truth
(southwest side)

'The next step on the path is led by the Spirit of Truth.' (Watts, p. 19) [Figs.77–78]

78

The symbolic bird

The bird of Truth is the owl, 'the bird of wisdom, whose eye can see through darkness' [Fig.78] (Watts, p. 19).

The central symbol

The central symbol is made up of the key, the labyrinth, the sun, the thunderbolt, and the Latin and Tau crosses.

> Over the starry universe is the key of truth, and in the key-bit is wrought the labyrinth where 'God leadeth,' and the path of light with its key to eternal life. The sceptre given to Truth is to this day used as a sign of sovereignty, in its origin probably a figure of the thunderbolt, the shaft being intended for the streak of lightning, while the ball represented the sun and the four cross winds of heaven, a summing-up of supreme supernatural power to the mind of primitive man. (Watts, p. 19)

The four attendant spirits

'The servants of Truth are Liberty, Justice, Unity and Law.' (Watts, p. 19)

79

The flying fish represents Liberty (inscription: 'LIBERTY'). [Fig.79] 'The flying fish, free in both air and sea, has been chosen as the type of Liberty' (Watts, p. 20). 'From the bondage of corruption into the glorious liberty of the children of God' (Romans 8:21).

80

The balance or scales represent Justice (inscription: 'JUSTICE'). [Fig.80] 'Justice follows with its balances; nothing false, nothing disproportionate, must take the path with the Spirit of Truth; and then the "Perfect Law of Liberty" comes in, a liberty of order, a perfect and just use of powers, in the least as in the greatest' (Watts, p. 20). Mary is referring to heavenly justice and the words of Christ: 'And, behold, there are last which shall be first, and there are first which shall be last' (Luke 13:30).

The seashell represents the Unity of the Universe (inscription: 'UNITY'). [Fig.81]

> The Unity of the Universe, the shell, of which Wordsworth says:–
>   'Far murmurings within were heard,
>   Mysterious union with its native sea.

81

> Even such a shell the universe itself
> Is to the ear of faith: and there are times,
> I doubt not, when to you it doth impart
> Authentic tidings of invisible things;
> Of ebb and flow, and ever during power,
> And eternal peace subsisting at the heart
> Of endless agitation. Here you stand
> Adore and worship when you know it not,
> Pious beyond the intention of your thought,
> Devout above the meaning of your will.'
> [William Wordsworth, *The Excursion* (1812), Book IV, 'Despondency Corrected, Sea Shell']
> (Watts, pp. 19–20)

82

The Scandinavian boat with a sun (right) and moon (left) represents the Law of the Universe (inscription: 'LAW'). [Fig.82] 'The Law of the Universe, for which the old Scandinavian of the boat, of the sun, and the moon has been chosen' (Watts, p. 19). Lindsay notes that the sun and moon in early Christian art symbolized the 'course of human life' (Lindsay, vol. I, p. xxi).

83

iii. Frieze of the Spirit of Love
(northwest side)

'From Truth the path leads on to Love, and on the north-west wall is the section where the Spirit of Love reigns.' (Watts, p. 20) [Figs.83–84]

84

The symbolic bird

The bird of Love is the pelican, 'the bird of … the legend, who draws blood from her own breast to feed her brood; a not uncommon representation of succouring, self-sacrificing love, and even of the King of Love Himself, in the religious architecture of the Middle Ages' [Fig.84] (Watts, p. 20). Audsley explains more fully its roots in early Christian art:

A figure of our Redeemer, often to be met with in early art, is the Pelican. It is represented surrounded with its young, and feeding them with its own blood. It is said that the Naturalists of old, observing that the Pelican had a crimson stain on its beak, reported that it was accustomed to feed its young with the flowing blood of its own breast, which it tore for the purpose. In this belief the early Christians adopted the Pelican to figure Christ, and set forth our redemption through His blood, which was willingly shed for us, His children. The Pelican was never invested with the nimbus, and, therefore, its place in art is not so exalted … Although the Pelican is beautiful and expressive figure of Christ, and cannot be too often used in modern work, we can scarcely claim for it a position as a symbol. (Audsley, pp. 40–41)

The central symbol

The central symbol is made up of hearts, circles, and the Latin and Tau crosses:

The central symbol, taken from a Celtic missal, enfolds a cross in the interlacing of its heart-shaped and circle-shaped curves; surely a fit cognizance to be borne by every traveller on the path that leads to perfect day. Of such a traveller an ancient hymn says:–

'This, too, is the goodness that he hath;
He lets his mind pervade one quarter of
   the world with thoughts of love,
And so the second,
And so the third,
And so the fourth,
And thus the whole wide world, above,
   below, around and everywhere,
Doth he continue to pervade with heart
   of love,
Far reaching, grown great, and beyond
   measure.'

[*Digha Nikaya* (The Long Discourses), trans. Thomas William Rhys Davis, ch. 13, verse 9] (Watts, pp. 20–21)

The four attendant spirits

The attendant spirits of Love are Purity, Peace, Joy and Service.

85

The heart-shaped lily represents purity (inscription: 'PURITY'). [Fig.85] 'On Love waits Purity, the symbol of the lily in the heart, "The white flower of a blameless life." [Alfred Tennyson, *The Idylls of the King*, dedication to the memory of Prince Albert] "As he thinketh in his heart, so is he" [Proverbs 23:7].' (Watts, p. 21)

The dove carrying an olive branch represents peace (inscription: 'PEACE'). [Fig.86] 'Peace:– The

86

dove, carrying the branch of olive, which symbol, when it is remembered how often trees and flowers are sown by birds who carry the seed, is beautifully amplified by the text: "The fruit of righteousness is sown in peace of them that make peace" [James 3:18].' (Watts, p. 21)

87

Bells represent joy (inscription: 'JOY'). [Fig.87] 'For Joy: the happy bells that "ring out the false" and "ring in the true" [from Alfred Tennyson's *In Memoriam*].' (Watts, p. 21)

88

The wheel represents service (inscription: 'SERVICE'). [Fig.88]

For Service, the service of God and the service of man. The wheel has been used as a symbol

89

for service – the wheel in its simplest form for the service of man, no aid of his own fashioning being more constantly in his service; and the winged wheel, with rays of light like whirling flames, for the symbol of the service of God – mystic, spiritual, eternal in its revolutions, from age to age, since light was first separated from darkness. In Ezekiel's visionary poetic words, 'As a wheel within a wheel,' [Ezekiel 1:16] may lie intimation of universal law, in which our earth resolves with suns and stars, in the service of the Creator. (Watts, pp. 21–22)

Lindsay identifies the wheel within a wheel as a familiar symbol of 'the two covenants' of 'the Old and New Testament' (Lindsay, vol. I, p. xxii). Furthermore, Mary used the image and words for the emblem of the Compton Pottery, recalling the words of Ezekiel, 'and their work was as it were a wheel in the middle of a wheel'.

iv. Frieze of the Spirit of Light
(northeast side)

'Finally the path ends in Light.' (Watts, p. 22) [Figs.89–90]

90

The symbolic bird

The bird of Light is the eagle. [Fig.90]

> The eagle who can look at the sun is the bird of Light; sometimes used as the symbol of the Holy Spirit, and also as the spirit of St John, who has declared the message to us, 'That God is Light, and in Him is no darkness at all' [1 John 1:5]. (Watts, p. 22)

91

The reference to St John is very marked as Audsley makes clear: 'The Eagle, as a symbol of the Spirit, is of very rare occurrence in Christian art, it being commonly employed to symbolize St John the Evangelist' (Audsley, p. 50). There is also a strong link with the image of the eagle of St John in the Book of Kells, [Fig.91] which is identical in form to Mary's symbolic bird. The dichotomy of darkness and light and the universal Word of God (Logos) are very much in evidence.

The central symbol

'The circle of a great light surrounded by other circles of suns and stars' (Watts, p. 22), evoking the Logos of the universe.

The four attendant spirits

The attendant spirits of Light are Godlike, Godward, Godlit and Godship.

92

The crescent moon and a Star of David represent Godlike, or heavenly temper (inscription: 'GODLIKE'). [Fig.92] 'In early Christian symbolism the crescent moon was the symbol of heaven.

It has been used here, with the word "God-like," to symbolize the heavenly temper. "Heaven is temper" wrote an English Divine, two centuries ago' (Watts, p. 22). Mary is recalling the words of Dr Thomas Chalmers (1780–1847), the Scottish mathematician and leader of the Free Church of Scotland who wrote, 'Heaven is a temper, not a place'. The crescent moon was very much an image of early Christian art, just as now it is mainly associated with Islam.

93

The flames of the five lamps of the watchful virgins represent rising to God, or Godward (inscription: 'GODWARD'). [Fig.93] The image of the lamps of the five wise virgins is taken from Matthew (25:3–4), in which: 'They that were foolish took their lamps, and took no oil with them: But the wise took oil in their vessels with their lamps'.

94

The eyes in a heart represent the divine eye of insight or Godlit (inscription: 'GODLIT'). [Fig.94] 'The word "God-lit," is suggested by the passage in Ephesians now in the revised version translation "Having the eyes of your heart enlightened, that we may know what is the hope of your calling," [Ephesians 1: 18] the divine eye of insight in the heart of man' (Watts, p.22).

95

The twelve flames of the Pentecostal shower represent inspiration or Godship (inscription: 'GODSHIP'). [Fig.95]

> For the flame of inspiration, the pentecostal shower, twelve flames descending upon the heads of those chosen messengers who were to carry the torch of the Gospel of Love. The flame of fire struck out, as if by miracle, from the dry wood, had for long ages seemed a heaven-born gift, and rising upward towards Heaven, as if drawn irresistibly thither and returning to its own, it became a beautiful and mystic symbol of the undying flame of life in the souls of the Sons of God. In token of this it was the primitive usage of the Church to put a lighted taper into the hand of the newly baptized. (Watts, pp. 22–23)

'And there appeared unto them cloven tongues like as of fire, and it sat upon each of them' (Acts 2:3).

96

97

5. The Belfry

The belfry stands above the south buttress and houses a 31 inch (79 cm) bell made by John Warner and Son of London. [Fig.97] It sounds the note 'C' and is inscribed with the words given by G.F. Watts, the donor of the chapel: 'Be my voice neither feared nor forgotten.' Its themes of remembrance, resurrection and consolation are to be found in its imagery. Its high position is seen as triumphant, the crowning 'for the conqueror who can rise above the lower plane of self-pity' (Watts, p. 24). On the north and south sides runs a frieze of doves holding an olive branch, 'signs of the presence of the Spirit of God speaking unutterable words of peace to the mourner' [Fig.96] (Watts, pp. 24–25). To the east and west are depicted 'wings rising out of the heart of a great seed husk, which, with the trumpet-shaped capitals of the small columns supporting the belfry roof are designed to suggest that ultimate word of triumph. "It is sown in weakness, it is raised in power" [1 Corinthians 15:4]' (Watts, p. 24). It also reflects the theme of resurrection in nature that Mary uses on the chapel's entrance.

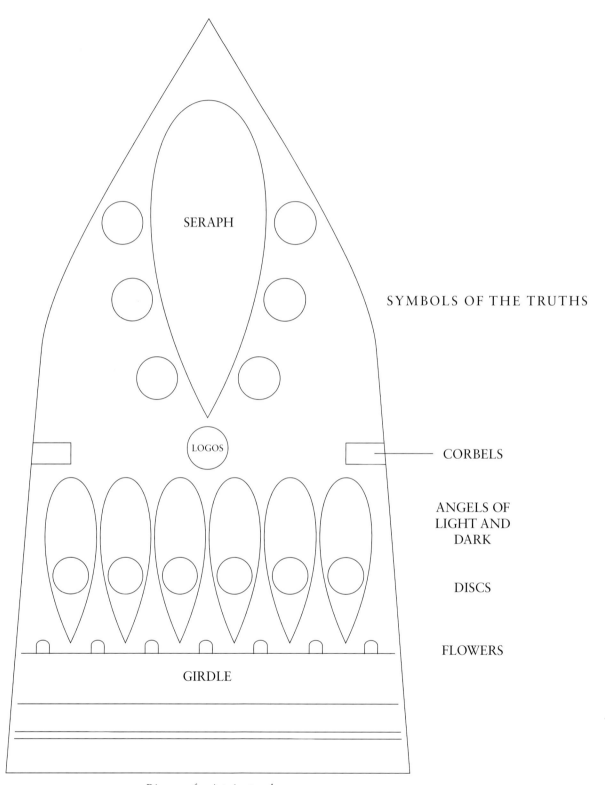

SERAPH

SYMBOLS OF THE TRUTHS

LOGOS

CORBELS

ANGELS OF
LIGHT AND
DARK

DISCS

FLOWERS

GIRDLE

Diagram of an interior panel

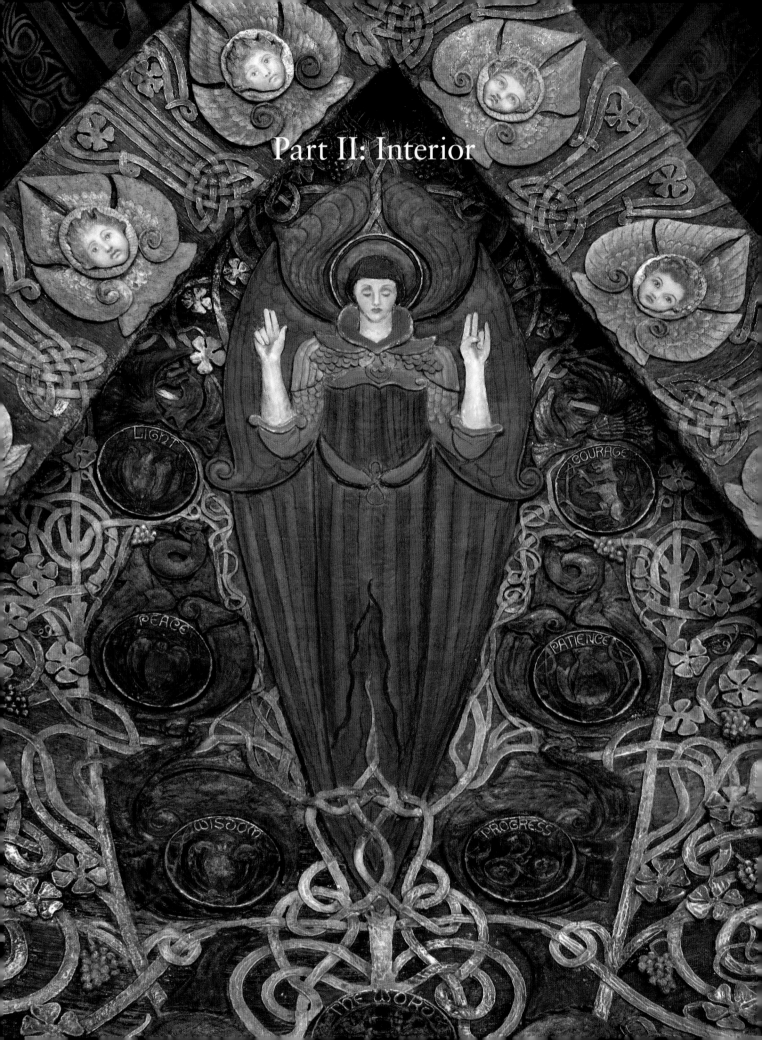

Part II: Interior

II. INTERIOR

6. Overall Design: Structure, Heaven and Earth, and Four Panels

A magic key … that unlocks a door into a world of enchantment (Watts, pp. 27–28)

i. The dome of heaven

Following the example of Byzantine churches, the cupola represents the dome of heaven rising from the earth. [Figs.98–99] As Lindsay notes, 'the Universe [is symbolized] by a globe or sphere, usually of deep blue' (Lindsay, vol. I, p. xix). Mary herself states: 'Of human life in its relation to Nature, rising towards "the Eternal relation of man with God," these patterns would speak' (Watts, p. 28).

In imitation of heaven there is a symbolic depiction of God at the very top: 'Over all, in the centre of the roof, in token of the unthinkable and the unspeakable Glory, is the circle of the eternal, without beginning, without end; the shelter of wings from everlasting to everlasting; the Infinite Love; the Sun of Righteousness' (Watts, p. 29). 'The Circle, or Ring, has been universally accepted as the emblem of eternity and perfect never-ending existence' (Audsley, p. 142). As the decorations move from God in heaven to the visitor on earth, the scheme follows a traditional early Christian hierarchy. Lindsay notes:

The heavenly host is divided (according to ecclesiastical authorities) into three hierarchies, and each hierarchy into three orders … To the Upper hierarchy belong the Seraphim, Cherubim and Thrones, dwelling nearest to God and in contemplation … To the Middle hierarchy – the Dominations, Virtues and Powers, – are committed the general government of the Universe, the gift of miracles in the cause of God … To the Lower – the Principalities, Archangels and Angels, – entrusted with the rule and ordinance of nations. (Lindsay, vol. I, pp. xxxiii–iv)

Mary's scheme follows this hierarchy in her depiction of angels.

99

ii. Angels

The Upper Hierarchy

Four seraphs
The four seraphs (the burning ones) represent the angels closest to God and are usually represented in red, as recorded in the book of Isaiah (6:1–7). 'The four Seraphs clothed in the crimson colour of love and life, with uplifted hands in sign

of a blessing' [Fig.98] (Watts, p. 29). Their hands are depicted in the act of a giving a blessing, one hand in the manner of the Greek or eastern church, one hand in the manner of the Latin or western church.

'Perhaps the most common form of the hand is that which represents it in the act of blessing. There are two forms of blessing to be found in art: one called the Greek, because it was adopted by the Eastern Church; the other the Latin, because it was adopted by Western Christians. [Fig.100] The difference lies only in the position of the fingers. The Greek form has the third finger bent towards the palm, and is crossed by the thumb, while the second and fourth fingers are curved inwards. This arrangement is symbolical of the name JESUS CHRIST, by representing four letters which begin and end the Sacred Name in Greek.' (Audsley, p. 30.) These are the letters 'I C X C', which stand as the first and last letters of Jesus Christ in Greek.

'The Latin benediction does not appear to represent letters, as in the Greek form, but to be purely symbolical. It shows the third and fourth fingers closed on the palm, leaving the thumb and first and second fingers extended. The arrangement is evidently intended to express the Trinity, in Whose name the benediction is given.' (Audsley, p. 31)

Cherubs [Figs.101–3]

Cherubs, like seraphs, are of the highest rank of angels and decorate the arches. They are described by Mary as 'a wreath of child-angel faces (one of the oldest symbols of the soul)' (Watts, p. 29). Cherubs appear in Genesis (4:24): 'So he drove out the man: and he placed at the east of the garden of Eden Cherubims and a flaming sword which turned every way, to keep the way of the tree of life'; and Ezekiel (28:14): 'Thou art the anointed cherub that covereth'. The corbels contain two phrases from the Apocrypha's book of Wisdom, verses traditionally used at memorial services: '[But] The Souls of the Righteous are in the hand of God [Wisdom 3:1] – their hope is full of immortality [Wisdom 3:4].' [Figs.104–11]

104

Corbel to the left of panel I

105

Corbel to the right of panel I

106

Corbel to the left of panel II

107

Corbel to the right of panel II

108

Corbel to the left of panel III

109

Corbel to the right of panel III

110

Corbel to the left of panel IV

111

Corbel to the right of panel IV

112

The Middle Hierarchy

The Dominations, Virtues and Powers
The Middle Hierarchy of heaven, which consists
of the 'Dominations, Virtues and Powers' that
are committed to the general government of the
universe, is loosely represented by the seven discs
that surround the seraphs (see p. 57). Six of the
discs contain 'the symbols of the truths which,
like the footprints of beneficent Creation, are
here to aid man in his search after the spiritual
existence' [Fig.112] (Watts, p. 29), while the seventh
is the Logos, or Word of God, from the prologue
of St John and is positioned under the seraph:

In the beginning was the Word.
The Word was with God.
The Word was God.
The Word was made flesh.

The Lower Hierarchy

Six spirits or winged messengers
The Lower Hierarchy of heaven and angels is
closer to earth, and Mary depicts twenty-four
'winged messengers', using a word that reflects
their Greek name *angelos* (messenger). [Fig.113]
They are divided into twelve pairs, in each of
which one faces outwards and the other inwards.
Mary explains them as follows:

The encircling group of winged messengers,
alternatively presenting the light and dark of
all things, 'made double one against the other,'
[Ecclesiasticus 42:23] would suggest the earthly
conditions in which the soul of man finds itself.

113

The face of the angel carrying the symbol of light
is seen, but the face of the angel carrying the
symbol of darkness is unseen. (Watts, pp. 28–29)

According to Lindsay, early Christian art ascribes

to the Lower – the Principalities, Archangels and
Angels, – entrusted with the rule and ordinance
of nations … every man being attended by two
angels, the one evil, persuading him to sin, for
the exercise of his faith, the other good, suggest-
ing righteousness and truth and protecting him
from the former. (Lindsay, vol. I, p. xxxiv)

114

iii. The Tree of Life

The whole of the interior is linked by the image of the Tree of Life whose roots and branches permeate the whole design. [Fig.114] 'The Tree of Life, spreading its all embracing branches against the blue of heaven, carries from root upwards the thought which inspired the design – the whole heaven as it were, into a mystical garment' (Watts, p. 28). The imagery of the tree, or vine, derives from the sources that are also used for the Life corbel on the outside of the chapel relating to St John and the Christian's life in Christ: 'Jesus said "I am the true vine, ye are the branches"' [Fig.115] (John 15:1, 5).

115

116

117

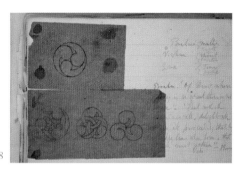

118

A terracotta band encircles the chapel like 'a golden girdle, into which the emblems of the Trinity are wrought' [Figs.116–17] (Watts, p. 28).

119

120

Just above the girdle 'the fair gifts of Nature are symbolised by little flowers' [Figs.119–20] (Watts, p. 28) created by the children of Compton.

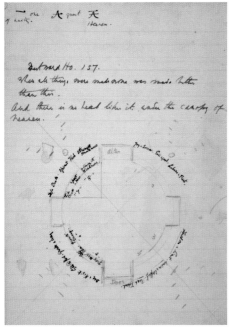

121

122

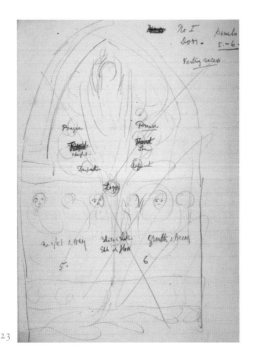

123

7. The Four Panels

The interior, like the outside and overall shape of the chapel, is divided into four parts or panels, as Mary describes them. Panel I begins to the left of the entrance, and they run clockwise to panel IV. Mary's sketchbooks show the changing ideas for the symbols of each of these. [Figs. 118, 121–23]

i. Discs of light and dark

The discs held by the angels are 'presenting the light and dark of all things', the positive and the negative, or the two sides of the same coin.

Panel I

In this panel Mary notes the theme of the symbols as 'universal in Nature' (Watts, p. 30) and in her notebook as the 'Gift of Nature'.

124

Day and night [Fig. 124]
Day is depicted by an angel holding the sun and inscribed 'Day' and 'Day unto Day uttereth speech'. Night is depicted as an angel in darkness and inscribed 'Day into night'.

Flow and ebb [Fig. 125]
Flow is depicted as a ship in full sail and inscribed 'Flow'. Ebb is depicted as a ship grounded and inscribed 'Ebb'.

125

126

Growth and decay [Fig.126]

Growth is depicted as a young naked child, opening outwards, growing. Decay is depicted as a clothed old man, curling inwards, decaying.

Panel II

In her notebook Mary describes the theme of the symbols in this panel as the 'Gift of God' and 'belonging not exclusively to the human being' (Watts, p. 30).

127

Life and death [Fig.127]

Life is depicted as a fragile figure being guided by love, the 'sail signifying the breath of life'. Death is depicted as the young woman gathering souls as flowers in her robes in G.F. Watts's painting *Time, Death and Judgement* and inscribed 'Death'.

128

Good and evil [Fig.128]

The subjects are taken from Christ's parable of the tares (Matthew 13:24–30, 36–40): 'The field is the world; the good seed are the children of the kingdom; but the tares are the children of the wicked one; The enemy that sowed them is the devil' (Matthew 13:38–39). Good is depicted as the sower planting the good seed. Evil is depicted as the enemy planting tares at night in the sowed field to ruin the crop.

129

Rest and labour [Fig.129]

Rest is depicted as a man reclining in a boat. Labour is depicted as a man carrying a boat on his back.

Panel III

In this panel Mary notes the theme of the symbols that 'belong exclusively to man' (Watts, p. 30).

130

Joy and sorrow [Fig.130]

Joy is depicted as a praising angel and sounding bells, the happy bells that ring out the false and ring in the true, and inscribed 'Joy'. Sorrow is depicted as an angel bent downwards filling a lachrymal or tear bottle.

131

Spirit and flesh [Fig.131]

Spirit is depicted as an invisible wind blowing (Greek *pneuma* meaning 'wind', 'breath' and 'spirit'). Flesh is depicted as a body laid in a tomb (or sarcophagus, which comes from the Greek *sarks* meaning 'flesh').

132

Ideal and Real [Fig.132]

The ideal is represented by a baby surrounded by the five senses. The baby has all the potential

to achieve the ideal before the senses dominate. Mary refers to this theme in her notebook as 'mental conception'. The real is depicted as the five disks of the senses holding back the ideal imagination. This theme is recorded in her notebook as 'sensuous perception'.

Panel IV

In her notebook Mary describes the theme of this panel's symbols as the 'Gift of Endeavour' and 'written large in the open book of nature' (Watts, p. 30).

133

Freedom and limit [Fig.133]

Freedom is depicted as a facing angel with a sunburst behind. Limit is depicted as an angel showing its back in a cloudy sky.

134

Union and conflict [Fig.134]

Union is depicted as a good and holy king. Conflict is depicted as a knight fighting a dragon.

Stability and change [Fig.135]

Stability is depicted as mountains with a sunburst behind it. Change is depicted as clouds being blown through the sky.

135

ii. The symbols of the truths

The four seraphs are surrounded by 'the symbols of the truths which, like the footprints of beneficent Creation, are here to aid man in his search after the spiritual existence'.

136

Panel I

'In the beginning was the Word' [Fig.136] (John 1:1).

137

Power is represented by an orb. [Fig.137] Babylonian and Egyptian in origin, the orb is used by the Byzantine Church with a cross, in which form it is one of the most familiar symbols of power used by monarchs.

138

Justice is represented by the scales of justice. [Fig.138]

139

Truth is represented by 'the boat of truth carrying the Sun with the sail signifying the breath of life' [Fig.139] (Watts, p. 30).

140

Unity is represented by 'the binding cord of unity' [Fig.140] (Watts, p. 30).

141

Order is represented by the 'the triskele [three conjoined spirals, particularly used in Celtic art] or three steps of the sun, morning, noon and night, while the outer circle has the sign of the four quarters of the earth or points of the compass' [Fig.141] (Watts, 2nd edition, p. 7).

142

Law is represented by the 'the ship of the Moon, the Measurer' [Fig.142] (Watts, p. 30).

143

Panel II

'The Word was with God' [Fig.143] (John 1:1).

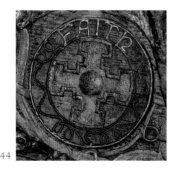

144

Faith is represented by the cross of faith, [Fig.144] the Greek cross, also the shape of the chapel.

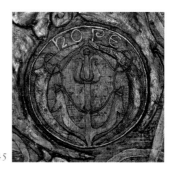

145

Hope is represented by the anchor of hope. [Fig.145]

146

Love is represented by the heart of love. [Fig.146]

147

Innocence is represented by the white flower in the heart of innocence. [Fig.147]

148

Obedience is represented by bees, symbolic of the law of the hive. [Fig.148]

149

Intuition is represented by the eye of the heart. [Fig.149]

150

Panel III

'The Word was God' [Fig.150] (John 1:1).

151

Mercy is represented by the eight-pointed cross of the Knights Hospitallers. [Fig.151]

Sacrifice is represented by the altar. [Fig.152]

152

153

Balance (or the finding of the golden mean) is represented by the scales, in which head and heart are of equal value. [Fig.153]

154

Inspiration is represented by the lamp. [Fig.154]

155

Aspiration is represented by the censer, regarded as a symbol, particularly in the Greek Orthodox Church. [Fig.155]

156

Meditation is represented 'by closed eyes, only the eye of the heart is open' [Fig.156] (Watts, p. 30).

157

Panel IV

'The Word was made flesh' (John 1:14). [Fig.157]

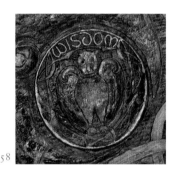

158

Wisdom is represented by the owl. [Fig.158]

159

Peace is represented by the dove. [Fig.159]

160

Light is represented by the eagle. [Fig.160]

161

Progress is represented by the wheel. [Fig.161]

162

Patience is represented by the brood hen. [Fig.162]

163

Courage is represented by the lion. [Fig.163]

iii. Flowers

There are thirty small stylized flowers modelled onto the four panelled walls by the children of Compton. These include the following:

Panel I

164

1. Mushroom [Fig.164]

165

2. Thistle [Fig.165]

Panel II

166

1. Poppy [Fig.166]

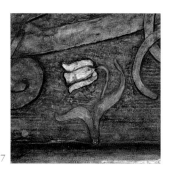

167

2. Snowflake [Fig.167]

Panel III

168

1. Crocus [Fig.168]

169

2. Lords and ladies [Fig.169]

Panel IV

170

1. Daffodil [Fig.170]

171

2. Nasturtium [Fig.171]

8. The Altar

i. The altar and its symbolism

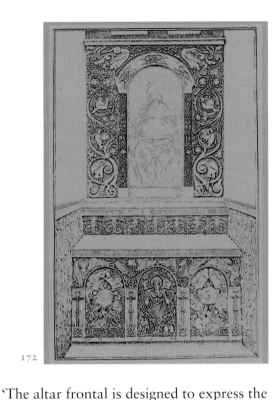

172

173

'Into the re-table is wrought a design representing the seven gifts of the spirit' (Watts, p. 31). Mary uses the traditional Christian image of seven doves to represent this. [Fig.173]

'The altar frontal is designed to express the words:– "I heard a great voice out of heaven, saying, The Tabernacle of God is with men; He shall dwell with them" [Revelation 21:3]' (Watts, p. 31). The words are interwoven into the decoration on the front of the altar, which is made in 'terra cotta, modelled in small panels. The designs are simple, but full of detail, and they are sufficiently varied to attract without fatiguing the eye of the worshipper' (Macmillan, p. 67). A drawing of its design was exhibited at the 1899 Home Arts and Industries exhibition held in the circular upper gallery of the Albert Hall. [Fig.172] The altar frontal is decorated with the four symbols of the Evangelists. Its central panels depict the Way, the Truth and the Life like the exterior corbels, but here Truth is represented by the human heart carried by an angel, and Life is shown as the three spirals of the Trinity.

174

Seven Doves are frequently depicted together, each one being in all respects similar to the single Dove, adopted to symbolize the Holy Ghost. These Doves represent the seven Spirits of God, the seven Gifts of the Spirit, or the one Holy Spirit in His sevenfold manifestations of Grace. The idea of the Spirits, which are thus set forth, is evidently derived from Scripture. [Figs.174–81] (Audsley, p. 48)

The Middle English spelling of the inscriptions that Mary uses to identify the gifts indicates a source such as Richard Rolle of Hampole's 'Seuene Gyftes of ye Haly Gaste'. They are as follows, with their name in modern English:

Wisdom: inscribed 'Ye gifte of wisdome'. [Fig. 175]

Piety: inscribed 'Ye gifte of pittie'. [Fig. 176]

Fortitude: inscribed 'Ye gifte of strengthe'. [Fig. 177]

Knowledge: inscribed 'Ye gifte of comfait'. [Fig. 178]

Understanding: inscribed 'Ye gifte of understandinge'. [Fig. 179]

Council (right judgement): inscribed 'Ye gifte of counyinge'. [Fig. 180]

181

Fear of the Lord (awe of God): inscribed 'Ye gifte of dreede'. [Fig.181]

182

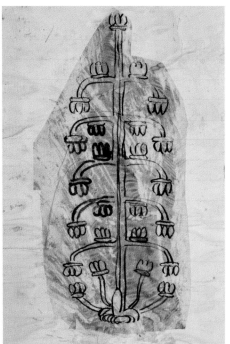

183

To either side of the altar are panels that represent the seven-branched candlestick. [Fig.182] 'And out of the throne proceeded lightenings and thunderings and voices: and there were seven lamps of fire burning before the throne, which are the seven spirits of God' (Revelation 4:5). This is one of the few images in Mary's chapel to be recognizably based on Egyptian designs. [Fig.183]

ii. The All-Pervading

The altar is dominated by a large G.F. Watts painting entitled *The All-Pervading*, [Figs.184–85] which was placed there on 15 April 1904, as Mary notes, 'when his own working days on this earth were so nearly accomplished' (Watts, p. 31). The painting had been conceived in the winter of 1887–88 when Watts was in Malta where he had observed the wonderful effects of a chandelier in his studio:

> To the unimaginative its glass drops and beads appeared to be the last thing in the world to suggest a picture … But he had found there some suggestion of the beautiful, and from it grew the solemn and mystic figure holding the universe in hands that encircle the sphere. (Watts Annals, vol. II, pp. 103–4)

The All-Pervading
by
G.F. Watts

184

The painting is now in the Tate and this smaller version was painted for the chapel, where it was seen by Watts; Mary reflected later: 'I am glad for-ever that he saw it' (Watts Annals, vol. II, p. 321).

185

It is a mysterious image of a hooded figure, reminiscent of Michelangelo's sibyls in the Sistine Chapel that look to the future. Watts saw the figure as 'the spirit that pervades the immeasur-able expanse' (Watts exhibition catalogue, New Gallery, 1896, no. 129). A globe, which represents the systems of the universe, its stars and galaxies, rests in the figure's lap, while a long scroll of the book of life is curved around his lap and legs. Mary notes that the globe contains 'the rush and Suns and roll of systems', a phrase taken from Tennyson's poem 'God and the Universe' (*Death of Oenone, Akbar's Dream, and Other Poems,* London 1892, p. 108):

> Must my day be dark by reason, O ye Heavens,
>   of your boundless nights,
> Rush of Suns, and roll of systems, and your
>   fiery clash of meteorites?

It is a powerful image of a creator that watches over and pervades the essence of everything, the Logos.

BIBLIOGRAPHY and ABBREVIATIONS

Abbreviations used in the text are given in **bold** *at the beginning of the relevant entry.*

ALLEN: J. Romilly Allen, *Early Christian Symbolism*, London 1887

J. ROMILLY ALLEN, 'Early Scandinavian Wood-Carvings, Part II', *The Studio*, 1897, pp. 82–90

J. ANDERSON and J. ROMILLY ALLEN, *Early Christian Monuments of Scotland*, Edinburgh 1903

ANON., 'A Remarkable Chapel, Erected from Designs by Mrs G.F. Watts', *The Graphic*, 22 July 1898

AUDSLEY: W. and G. Audsley, *A Handbook of Christian Symbolism*, London 1865

WILFRID BLUNT, *'England's Michelangelo': A Biography of George Frederic Watts, O.M., R.A.*, London 1975

LOUISE BOREHAM, 'Compton Chapel', *The Victorian: Magazine of the Victorian Society*, no. 3, March 2000, pp. 10–13.

BRINDLEY & WEATHERLEY: W. Brindley and W.S. Weatherley, *Ancient Sepulchral Monuments*, London 1887

VERONICA FRANKLIN GOULD, *Watts Chapel: An Arts & Crafts Memorial*, privately published, 1993

VERONICA FRANKLIN GOULD, *Mary Seton Watts, 1849–1938: Unsung Heroine of the Art Nouveau*, Compton 1998

VERONICA FRANKLIN GOULD, *Archibald Knox and Mary Seton Watts: 'Modern Celtic Art' Garden Pottery*, privately published, 2001

H. HILDEBRAND, *The Industrial Arts of Scandinavia in Pagan Times*, London 1883

WILLIAM LETHABY, *Architecture, Mysticism and Myth*, London 1891

LINDSAY: Lord Lindsay, *Sketches of the History of Christian Art*, 3 vols., London 1847

MACMILLAN: Hugh Macmillan, *The Life-Work of George Frederick Watts, R.A.*, London 1903

RICHARD ROLLE OF HAMPOLE, 'The Seven Gifts of the Holy Ghost', in Kenneth Sisam, ed., *Fourteenth Century Verse and Prose*, Oxford 1921, pp. 42–43

GEORGE SMITH, *The History of Babylonia*, ed. Revd A.H. Sayce, London 1884

STOKES: Margaret Stokes, *Early Christian Art in Ireland*, London 1887

J. STUART, *Sculptured Stones of Scotland*, London 1867

THE STUDIO: An Illustrated Magazine of Fine and Applied Art, London 1893–1964

MARY WATTS, 'Chapel Notebook', Watts Gallery Archive

MARY WATTS, Diaries and Various Papers, Watts Gallery Archive

WATTS: Mary Watts, *The Word in the Pattern* (manuscript *c.* 1899), London 1905: 1st and 2nd editions reprinted in 1998 (1st edition is used in references unless stated otherwise)

WATTS ANNALS: Mary Watts, *George Frederic Watts: The Annals of an Artist's Life*, 3 vols., London 1912

JOHN OBADIAH WESTWOOD, *Fac-similies of the Miniatures and Ornaments of Anglo-Saxon and Irish Manuscripts*, London 1868

J. GLEESON WHITE, 'A Mortuary Chapel. Designed by Mrs G.F. Watts', *The Studio*, 1898, pp. 235–40

SHELAGH WILSON, 'Watts, women, philanthropy and the home arts', in Colin Trodd and Stephanie Brown, eds., *Representations of G.F. Watts: Art Making in Victorian Culture*, Aldershot 2004

J.J.A. WORSAAE, *The Industrial Arts of Denmark: From the Earliest Times to the Danish Conquest of England*, London 1882

Compton Cemetery Chapel